QUEEN'S

PARK

255ª
30·034

B.M. 158·8

B.M. 136·6

B.M. 126·9

B.M. 124·2

B.M. 120·7

B.M. 118·9

B.M. 117·1

B.M. 107·8

Public Library
Fire Station
Willesden L. B. Offices
Mortuary
Police Station

Queen's Park
Station

L.B

S.B

ALBERT GARDEN

B.M. 111·9

CLAREMONT ROAD

Fn.

B.M. 116·2

B.Se

Hotel

St. Luke's
Church

(Det.)
(Det.)

MORTIMER ROAD

B.M. 120·5

LONDON & NORTH WESTERN RAILWAY

B.M. 129·7

B.M. 115·0

ALLINGTON STREET

KILBURN LANE

Laundry

B.Se

Chap

School

School

Chamberlayne
Farm

B.M. 105·3

School

Chap

L.B

BEETHOVEN STREET

108·8

NUTBOURNE STREET

B.M. 116·0

L.B. School

L.B.

B.M. 106·0

B.M. 109

MARBAN ROAD

MARNE STREET

DART STREET

B.M. 105·5

LOTHROP STREET

KILRAVOCK STREET

B.M. 112·6

PEACH STREET

B.M. 111·5 S

Institute

B.M. 108·1

MOZART STREET

B.M. 100·6

John's
Church

School

FARRANT STREET

B.M. 104·8

CAIRD STREET

B.M. 102·0

HUXLEY STREET

GALTON STREET

FOURTH AVENUE

ENBROOK STREET

School

SECOND AVENUE

BARRETT STREET

ALPERTON STREET

FIRST AVENUE

GODMARNE ROAD

P.L.
B.M. 98·7

Church
Place

B.M. 100·3

B.M. 92·9

Kensington
Wharf

Mission Hall

P.H.

Methodist
Chapel

P.H.

St. Thomas's
Church

JUNCTION CANAL PADDINGTON BRANCH

B.M. 98·6

Public
Library

B.M. 97·8

P.O.

Cottage

2·790

B.M. 101·1

B.M. 101·2

B.Se

P.L.

QUEEN'S PARK

KENSAL, BRONDESBURY AND HARLESDEN

A Pictorial History

Here is Willesden Lane by the corner with Winchester Avenue, in about 1906, near the bridge over the North London Line, which shows the heavy style of building loved by Victorian developers – four storeys and a basement. At number 143, the corner house, was Brondesbury College. The Principal was Mr P.H. Happerfield. In the distance the spire of Christ Church rises high on this rather dull day in October. In the 1960s, the radical Willesden Council sought to improve much of the run-down housing and replaced this block with Mapes House and other blocks of flats.

QUEEN'S PARK

KENSAL, BRONDESBURY AND HARLESDEN

A Pictorial History

Len Snow

Phillimore

2006

Published by
PHILLIMORE & CO. LTD
Shopwyke Manor Barn, Chichester, West Sussex, England
www.phillimore.co.uk

© Len Snow, 2006

ISBN   1-86077-416-4
ISBN 13   978-1-86077-416-4

Printed and bound in Great Britain by
THE CROMWELL PRESS
Trowbridge, Wiltshire

List of Illustrations

Frontispiece: Willesden Lane near Winchester Avenue, 1906
xii: Map of Queen's Park and District, 1904

Queen's Park

Kensal Green and Kensal Rise

Brondesbury

Harlesden

Acknowledgements

My most grateful thanks are to Tina Morton and the staff at the Brent Local Archive for access to their excellent store of illustrations. They were always at hand to assist and answer every question – which they did from their great store of knowledge of our Borough and its excellent Archive. The illustrations form the bulk of those contained in the book and they are all those not otherwise listed. London's Transport Museum, at Transport for London, for no. 42; London Metropolitan Archive: Nos 6 and 7; Images of London: 4, 5, 14, 26, 32, 41, 45, 49, 87, 107, 108, 110, 113, 114, 116, 118, 122, 151, 152; Guildhall Library, City of London: No. 85; City of Westminster Archives Centre: 175, 176, 177, 178, 180, 181, 182, 183, 184, 184, 185, 186. The end-papers and no. 183 are reproduced from Ordnance Survey maps © Crown Copyright; the map on p. xii is reproduced by permission of Stanfords.

My other big 'thank you' is to Cliff Wadsworth from whose collection of monographs on Willesden I have drawn frequently – his unceasing search for knowledge of our parish is astounding and an example to other local historians.

For the Queen's Park Estate, I am grateful to Rory Lalwan and the staff of the Westminster City Archive Centre, staff of Queen's Park Library and to Erica McDonald and David J. Smith, authors of *Artizans and Avenues,* a history of the Queen's Park estate, for permission to make use of their intensive research into the history of the Estate contained in their book.

I owe a continuing debt of gratitude to my publishers, Phillimore and Co., for their faith in me and especially to Noel Osborne and Rebecca Harris, and to Sarah Kiddle, Peter Cook and Nicola Willmot who made exciting sense out of the plain black and white script and illustrations.

As always, my wife Joan and daughter Susan have been just wonderful all the way through with advice and help, Susan especially with the continuing complexities of computers.

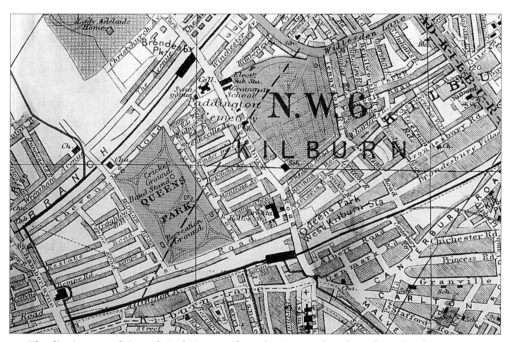

The district around Queen's Park, in 1904, from the Bacon Atlas of London. The elegant estate around it is not quite completed, but its final shape is evident. To the east, Kilburn had been developed in the 1870s to 1890s and was the thriving heart of the new Wilesden Council.

Introduction

'From the Fountain to the Clock' could be the florid, fascinating and factual subtitle for this book. The fountain is in Queen's Park, which was opened in 1887, Queen Victoria's Golden Jubilee year, as was the Jubilee Clock at Harlesden.

The areas of Willesden (now Brent) covered – Queen's Park, Kensal Rise and Kensal Green, Brondesbury and Harlesden – are districts that have various, changeable boundaries – parish or council. However, people who live there know exactly where they live and if one district shades into another it is not serious – you are where you are.

Willesden was and is a place of great contrasts. There were soggy marsh lands and tree-topped hills; manor houses and slums; rich bankers and poor farm-workers. Above all, people lived here for thousands of years, proudly parochial, discreetly devout.

Willesden parish probably dates back to around A.D. 938. It contains Harlesden, which has its own Domesday entry; other village areas such as Kensal Green and Kensal Rise can be dated to the 13th century – and there is Queen's Park, which is very definitely of the 19th century.

Place names are not only fascinating. They contain a wealth of historical information in each word. **Willesden** – like many place names in England Anglo-Saxon – derives from two words that mean 'the hill of the spring' and they refer to Mount Pleasant, rising above the land that was to become Willesden Green, with a stream flowing from the spring down to the Slade Brook and on to the River Brent. **Kensal** means 'King's Holt', referred to in a document of 1253, although there is no clue as to which king or which date might be involved or when it was established. **Brondesbury** manor takes its name from Prebendary Brand (*c.*1192-1215). **Harlesden** is 'Herewulf's tun', which is 'Herewulf', a local Saxon tribal leader, and 'tun', an enclosure or farmstead. **Queen's Park** is easy – it refers to Queen Victoria, no less.

Like so many present-day suburbs of London, the district was a quiet rural area of farms and small villages within boundaries: the River Brent on the west, the old Roman road, Watling Street, on the east and, on the southern edge, a less easily identifiable route along the Kilburn stream, across fields to the Brent again. Close as it was to London, it remained almost cut off, as a rural enclave, until the arrival first of the canal and then of the mainline railway, which brought the urban world to its doorstep.

The few early residents of Kilburn, neighbour to Queen's Park, stretching along Watling Street and the Edgware Road, were stimulated by the continuous procession of traffic of all kinds, from horses to horse-drawn vehicles, to provide inns and hostelries – as well as the famous Kilburn Priory – to cater for the travellers. Kensal Green benefited from the activity on a lesser but still important road to Harrow. Then, the creation of All Souls' Cemetery at Kensal Green in 1832 – which, although it is actually outside the borough has a strong connection with its neighbour – generated a buzz of activity along its little stretch of greenery. Harlesden's existence as a separate village within Willesden parish is attested to by its entry in Domesday Book. It was a little further along the road to Harrow than Kensal Green and saw itself well placed to cater for the needs of travellers with several inns like the *Crown* and the *Green Man*. It also saw growth emerging when the railway came through Willesden Junction.

Willesden, including the southern area that is covered in this history, may have seen some of the nomadic Celtic tribes who left relatively few traces of their existence, at least in this area of old Middlesex. The simple evidence that there were Britons here is to be found in the river names, which were handed down by word of mouth – Thames and Brent locally and many others across England. There is no evidence that, at the time of Julius Caesar's invasions, there were any settled Celtic tribes in Middlesex.

There is very little evidence of Roman occupation in Willesden. In 2002 excavations on the Thames Water facility on Dollis Hill uncovered a possible farm building. However, there is the most important remain of all – Watling Street, the straight Roman road from Dover to London and on to St Albans, Shrewsbury and perhaps beyond to Wales. It has been the established border of Willesden for a thousand years and was even, for a short period, the border between King Alfred's Wessex and the Danelaw – wild border country indeed.

With the withdrawal of Roman forces to Rome in A.D. 410, the vacuum thereby created was soon filled by marauding bands of Angles, Saxons and Jutes at first probing to see what the country was like. (They had been carrying out raids for a hundred years past, but never settled.) Thus, slowly, over several hundred years, tribes found likely plots of land they could exploit and cultivate. With this permanency came a name. Often it was the obvious choice – the head of the tribe or family: thus Herewulf in the subsequent Harlesden, or Wemba whose clearing or *leah* gave us Wembley. Other names came from the physical feature: Willesden has already been explained; Neasden is 'the nose-shaped hill'; Kilburn 'the stream of cattle' – all are Anglo-Saxon in origin.

As the battling tribal chiefs and kings settled into some sort of mutual peace, areas like Mercia, Northumbria and Wessex in turn dominated England and the latter, under Alfred, came to rule the whole country – other than the large eastern part that for a period came under Danish (Viking) rule. The manors (or *mansae*), into which Willesden and other districts were divided, were first adumbrated around A.D. 938, though a document detailing them, signed supposedly by Alfred's grandson Athelstan, is now considered spurious. Harlesden is one of these, as is Chamberlayne, Bounds (on the south-east border of Willesden) and seven others. (They were represented by absentee 'landlords', who were prebendaries of St Paul's Cathedral, who were entitled to a seat in the cathedral chancel – with the names of their prebends still enshrined on the mahogany benches.)

Thus it remained, with its score or so of families, for hundreds of years with very little change to the quiet, bucolic way of life. Ownership of the land during the centuries following the compilation of Domesday Book is lovingly catalogued in *The Victoria County History for Willesden*. This tells us little about the ordinary people but records, for example, a prebendary around 1215, Gilbert de Plesseto, who granted most of Harlesden to his co-prelate Richard de Camera, who gives his name to the neighbouring manor of Chamberlayne. Some time later it must have reverted, as it is known to have been leased to the Roberts family, particularly Edmund in 1576. (His tombstone is in Willesden Church.) They also held, indeed ruled, Neasden for many years.

In 1841 the population of Willesden was over 3,500 and, even by the 1851 census, Kensal village was larger than Kilburn. (The High Road Station was only opened that year and it took several years for it to become popular as a link to the city.) The two were separated by farms such as George Hodson's 150 acres and Bannister's, though these were severed by the London & Birmingham Railway in 1837 and were taken over for housing developments – hence Bannister Road. *Kelly's Directory* for 1845 records horse-drawn omnibus services including one daily from the *Royal Oak* at Harlesden through Kensall [*sic*] Green at 9, 11, 2, 4, 6, and 8 o'clock. To take transport one small stage further, in 1888, the first horse-drawn tramway in north-west London was built for the short distance from Amberley Road Paddington to Harlesden Green, with a depot in Trenmar Gardens College Park. The fare was twopence all the way. For a weekly wage of 5s. 9d. the drivers sat in their open cabs, their moustaches freezing in the winter chill or boiling in the summer sun.

In the 1870s Kensal was still part of the rural area of Willesden, in contrast with the urbanised Kilburn. One of the distinguishing features was that Kensal's houses drained into open privies, while Kilburn's drained into the metropolitan sewers. In the struggle for local democracy, Kensal sided with Harlesden, but they lost out when the decision was made to grant local board status to Willesden in 1875. Then Kensal began to stretch out towards Kilburn, feverishly overwhelming the farmlands, while Kilburn equally spread frantically westwards until eventually they met, thus covering southern Willesden with a network of houses – always excepting the glorious open spaces of Queen's Park and the long-existing Paddington Cemetery. In the triangle between the Harrow Road and the railway, developers like the United Land Company acquired land from All Souls' College and set to work. The road names give the game away – Hazel was the land agent for the college, Purves a solicitor of the land company. Wakeman was another farmer who sold out, unable to withstand the flow of bricks and mortar. Halstow and Rainham are the names of All Souls' estates in Kent and Pember was a fellow of the college.

The Victorian author Harrison Ainsworth came to live at Kensal Manor House, having lived at Kensal Lodge from 1835 to 1841, until 1853. (Both houses are no longer standing.) Here he wrote many of his most successful novels and entertained his many friends who were themselves part of the literary circle of the time – Dickens, Thackeray and John Forster among them.

Kensal Green also stretched north, up the hill, to become Kensal Rise, where another local railway strained to reach Willesden Junction and, on succeeding, helped create that mysterious warren with a facility for helping passengers get lost, as the novelist Trollope proclaimed. Here, the roads reflect the ecclesiastical connection – prebendaries of St Paul's like Kempe, Millman and Peploe.

An early Women's Co-operative Movement branch was started in Chamberlayne Road in 1887 and soon after a Co-op shop was opened. (Sadly it is no longer there.) Many of the houses were built by Charles Langler and Charles Pinkham (who became a stalwart of the Middlesex County Council, then an MP and was knighted. He had a section of the north circular road named after him – Pinkham Way.)

Before the houses overwhelmed the district, a national athletic ground was laid out in 1890 in the fields just north of Kensal Rise Station, where Clifford, Leigh and Whitmore Gardens are now. Queen's Park Rangers Football Club had been formed in that part of Queen's Park that is also known as West Kilburn. It had quite a number of bases in its early years and this athletic ground was one of them.

As Kensal developed it included the necessary features of a good town. Shops punctuated Chamberlayne Road (built by All Souls' College on the line of an existing footpath to facilitate the developments) up to Kensal Rise Station. Churches were always an early mark of the parish: St John's is at the corner of the Harrow Road and Kilburn Lane, actually in Paddington but serving the whole community. When Mortimer Road was built (its eastern half later renamed Harvist Road) the Ecclesiastical Commissioners left space and from St John's the Christ Church mission was set up there, but the name was later changed to St Martin. St Lawrence in Chevening Road and St Anne's in Salusbury Road – the two were later amalgamated on the latter's site – were, with St Martin, all built by the brothers Cutts. The Jewish community, slowly expanding, had as one of its leaders a master-builder, who developed much of Kilburn. He was Solomon Barnett, who also helped build the Brondesbury Synagogue in Chevening Road.

Schools were at first provided by the Church of England, some of which have not lasted, like St John's at Kensal Green. More successful were Keble Memorial in Crownhill Road, Harlesden and Princess Frederica in Purves Road – both sponsored by Emily Ayekbown – and Christ Church on Willesden Lane, the brainchild of Dr Williams, the rector of the church in Brondesbury. There were a number of private schools, some of which had no longer a lease of life than some of the church schools. One such was Henley House in Mortimer Road where, around 1880, the head teacher was J. Vine Milne, the father of A.A. Milne the author of *Winnie the Pooh*, and the science teacher was H.G. Wells, also to become a world-famous author.

The Roman Catholic diocese opened the Convent School of Jesus and Mary (next door to Keble) and later Cardinal Hinsley in Harlesden Road. The author's own secondary school, Kilburn Grammar, on Salusbury Road, founded by Dr Bonavia Hunt, began in 1898 in Willesden Lane before moving to its later premises, opposite the Brondesbury and Kilburn Girls' High School – both schools now successfully taken over as Muslim schools. The boys' school claims amongst its many well-known alumni Richard Baker of broadcasting fame, while the girls' school can proudly claim the model and actress Twiggy (Lesley Hornby) and Gwen Molloy, the local historian. From one of the classrooms at my school we could, surreptitiously, look out on Paddington Cemetery, which, some time after my fevered glances took place, was acquired by Brent Council from Westminster for the princely sum of £1.

Once the district had been fully built up, the time came – as it always seems to do – for its renewal. Following the Council's practice of redeveloping whole estates such as South Kilburn and Church End, the same tactic was applied to Kensal Green. This time the residents rose in revolt and rejected the council's feeble proposals, opting instead for rehabilitation. The multi-ethnic community spoke with one voice to assert its rights and the pleasant streets of Felixstowe and Ravensworth Roads, Victor and Napier continue to shine forth with rugged owner-occupier pride.

Queen's Park and Brondesbury

Long before Queen's Park was conceived, Brondesbury (or Brands) Manor was one of the prebendal manors created by the Dean and Chapter of St Paul's who held the land, which they then farmed or leased out. Subsequently the Ecclesiastical Commissioners (now the Church Commissioners) took it over and, in the 19th century, like other large landlords, decided to follow the trend and sell off land for development for housing.

In 1879 the Royal Agricultural Society, looking for a suitable site for their annual show, found a large site in Willesden on the lower part of the slope from the Brondesbury Ridge. In July the farming world came to Kilburn, led by Queen Victoria and the Prince of Wales (later Edward VII), who opened it on the one fine day of that month. Unfortunately, the summer that year was exceptionally bad and it rained so much that Kilburn and the show became synonymous with mud. It was served by Kensal Rise Station to the north (then called Kensal Green) and the newly built station on the line from Euston, then called Queen's Park & West Kilburn (and now of course Queen's Park).

A few years later a campaign was started to open a park on the site. The Corporation of London was sympathetic but had to organise the funding when, suddenly in 1885, the Ecclesiastical Commissioners offered the site (along with Highgate Wood) to the City of London as a gift 'for the preservation as open spaces for ever'. The Willesden Local Board congratulated them. The corporation were at first rather unwilling to take both, claiming shortage of funds, but a timely benefaction from the bequest of William Ward 'for the creation of some fund for the benefit of the poorer classes' enabled them to accept. An Act of Parliament was passed in 1886 and the open space was laid out at a cost to the corporation of some £3,000. It was named Queen's Park in honour of the Golden Jubilee of Victoria and opened by the Lord Mayor on 5 November 1887 'for the free use and enjoyment of the public for ever'. The surrounding area was used for housing, starting with Kingswood Avenue on the east and roads running towards Salusbury Road.

There is also shown on some maps a pathway called Brand's Causeway, roughly along the present Brondesbury Park. The land seems to have reverted in 1840 to the Ecclesiastical Commissioners, the ubiquitous owners of much of Willesden, but for many years it was owned by the Marsh family. In 1788 it was bought by Lady Sarah Salusbury (thus establishing the key road name in the area). The manor house is described as a moated house in 1538, rebuilt at various times and, by the time of Lady Salusbury, was a three-storeyed villa with landscaping carried out by the great Humphry Repton (who also worked on Wembley Park). In the 19th century it was occupied by Sir Coutts Trotter and

Charles Hambro, among others. Then, after being empty, it became a school from 1882 to 1934, when it was bought by a local builder, C.W.B. Simmonds, pulled down and is now the still-fashionable Manor House Drive.

In the 1850s, Brondesbury Ridge was regarded as a highly desirable place to live, outside London but with fine views of the Surrey Hills and a bright clear atmosphere. No wonder the Ecclesiastical Commissioners in 1847 rubbed their hands with glee at the prospect of converting rather dull ordinary agricultural land into profitable building land (and from then on refused to allow new public houses to be built on the land they gave up for development). Cavendish Road (where it was alleged some builders used mud from the road mixed with their cement for their brickwork!) and Brondesbury Park as well as Willesden Lane, right on the rise of the ridge, all saw charming villas built, a few of which are still in use and cheerfully provide homes, or in some cases schools or other institutions. The Victorian adventure writer W.H.G. Kingston lived here in Stormont House and his name is commemorated in a block of flats in The Avenue.

Confusing to some is Queen's Park in Paddington (now Westminster), on the south side of Kilburn Lane, also known as West Kilburn. To try to overcome any doubts I have included a small section describing the fascinating development of this Victorian housing estate, which shares a common boundary with its namesake as well as the railway station.

Kensal

There was never a manor house in the manor of Chamberlayne Wood. It drew its name from Richard de Camera (the Latin version of 'chamber') who was the prebendary in the early 13th century and also rector of St Mary's Willesden. It was closely associated with its neighbouring manors of Bounds or the Rectory Manor (which, although on the eastern edge of the parish, was regarded as the leading manor and had its manor house on Kilburn High Road between Oxford Road and Cambridge Avenue) and Brondesbury Manor to the north.

The complicated exchange of leases and purchases of land is carefully and diligently explored in the *Victoria County History* mentioned earlier, and I will simply summarise the overall impression: 'sub-manors' were created, such as Malorees and Kingsholt (which became Kensal). Malorees appears to have taken its name from Peter Malourie and the territory extended into Chelsea.

The main change that occurred, in 1438, was the conveyance of much of this area of Willesden to Thomas Chichele (Archbishop of Canterbury 1414-43), who founded All Souls' College, which, through his benefaction, acquired these lands. Incidentally, as the estates were later developed for housing, the road names reflected the college connection: Chichele Road, All Souls' Avenue, College Road and a score of others with names of Fellows of All Souls' such as Anson and Dicey.

Interestingly, Kensal (Kingsholte) and Kingsbury share a little royal mystery. Their names both refer to a king, but which, and why a fort or a wood respectively? The likeliest explanation is that they refer to royalty's fondness for hunting and that these were resorts near London used for such an exercise. Another little coincidence arises with Chamberlayne Wood and Kingsholte (i.e. King's Wood) – two small woods, one possibly named for a king and another for one of his court officers, a chamberlain. One more puzzle is that, on John Roque's 1745 map of London, there is listed 'Stonebridge Wood' lying between Harlesden and Kensal Green – though it is clearly not linked to the Stonebridge that derives from the crossing of the Brent in the south-west corner of Willesden.

Apart from these woods, the district was farmland leased either from the Church or from All Souls' College. An illustration of what Kensal might have been like in 1665 comes from the exciting novel *Old St Paul's* by Harrison Ainsworth. This tells the story of the Great Plague in London and, at one point in the plot, his characters flee from London passing through Paddington (then a small village), travel along the Harrow Road (passing a large pest-house for victims of the plague) and reach a small farmhouse at the summit of the hill. There they stay with the farmer named Wingfield whose daughter had just died of a broken heart and was buried in Willesden churchyard (where there is a tombstone to a family of the same name – presumably seen by Ainsworth). 'A pleasant walk across the fields brought them to the pretty village of Willesden and its old and beautiful church. They proceeded to the grave of poor Sarah Wingfield which lay at the east of the church beneath one of the tall elms.' However, it is only a story, like Ainsworth's romance about the highwayman Jack Sheppard.

The road that bounded them on the southern side was the badly kept, but important, road out of London to Harrow, a seat of the Archbishop of Canterbury – in other words, the Harrow Road as we know it. As early as 1550 the green existed and it stretched westwards from the junction with Kilburn Lane (in the 17th century known as Flowerhills Lane, but marked with its current name on John Roque's 1745 map). Two farm houses are shown on the Roque map, one on the south side later to be absorbed into Kensal Green Cemetery, which may have included the *Plough* public house. The *Plough* was one of the haunts of the painter George Morland and recent research suggests that it was the one in Kilburn Lane that he frequented. (Kilburn Lane was then a footpath to Kilburn Priory.)

The Brent Archives (Mr M.C. Barres-Baker) have identified that, after 1814, the green was used as a shooting range by the Cumberland Sharpshooters, a local rifle club – not the first and certainly not the last of such sporting societies. The Willesden Steeplechases were held a little further north on ground that is now the King Edward VII Recreation Ground (and Willesden Sports Centre), between Donnington Road and Doyle Gardens.

In 1801, the Paddington Branch of the Grand Union (later Grand Junction) Canal came very close to Kensal Green and, along its length at various villages, Alperton, Harlesden, Kensal and so on, brick works were established, using the convenient form of transport for the handling of the raw materials and the finished bricks. Children from the farms would run down to see the barges moving along and farmers also used it to bring in foodstuffs for their animals and to send hay into London.

One of the decidedly unwelcome effects of the 1815 Enclosure Act for Willesden was the loss of Kensal Green, small as it was, and cottages were built on the plots created out of its demise. Regent Street (the Brent one) was presumably built at about this time, recalling the then Prince of Wales' role in the last decade of his illustrious father George III. Some of these are still there along the Harrow Road, with other, slightly more substantial villas built opposite the forbidding wall of the now famous All Souls' Cemetery, the correct name for the more familiar Kensal Green Cemetery, which lies in today's Royal Borough of Kensington & Chelsea.

Harlesden

These early, small communities were farming centres, hardly growing over hundreds of years. Harlesden has its own entry in Domesday Book of 1086: 'The Canons [i.e. of St Paul's] hold Harlesden as one manor. It answers for 5 hides. Land for 4 ploughs. In lordship 2 ploughs. The villagers ½ plough; 1½ ploughs possible. 12 villagers with 1 virgate each; 10 villagers with ½ virgate each. Woodland, 100pigs. In total value 35s; when acquired the same; before 1066 £4. The manor was in the lordship of the Canons of St Paul's before 1066 and still is.' (Phillimore edition of *Domesday Book: Middlesex*, translated by John Morris, 1975.)

In simple terms what this means is that the manor of Harlesden was about 600 acres (taking a hide as about 120 acres). 'In lordship' refers to the amount of land reserved for the owner (in this case St Paul's) to use; the rest the villagers shared. The 22 villagers might suggest, with their families, a population of about 100 – it was a middling-sized village at that time.

As happened with all properties, Harlesden changed hands over the years, leaving the farm workers, smiths and innkeepers to carry on undisturbed. The green was a prominent part of the village with the manor house – a rather grand name for what was little more than a cottage. For many years, the green extended from what was later All Souls' Church along to the later Wrottesley Road, the manor house sitting in the centre near the *Royal Oak* and looking down the Harrow Road towards Scrubs Lane. To the north of the manor house (as Simeon Potter tells us in his early book *The Story of Willesden*) were fields with names such as New Close, the Pightle (which means a small enclosure), Lower and Upper Field, Lucy's Croft (we still have The Croft, off Harlesden High Street, though without the girl's name included) and Home Mead. Further to the north – and now within Roundwood Park – were Knowle's Shot and Hunger Hill Common Field. The road to Harrow, which came from Paddington Green through to Harrow on the Hill, wound its way round field boundaries so that even today it twists and turns at the *Royal Oak*, at the Jubilee Clock and, until the early 19th century, turned sharp left at the start of Church Road before straightening out by St Michael's Church.

In the 17th century, the Taylor family acquired the Harlesden manor and lessees later included the Wright and Sellon families, remembered in modern street names.

The building of the Grand Junction Canal a little to the south of the village and, as mentioned earlier, the coming of the railway in 1837 began the lifting of the district from rural poverty towards urban improvements. The gangs of (mostly) Irish labourers ('navvies' – from navigation canals) brought a minor wave of immigrants into Brent. With the opening of its own railway station, a tiny halt staffed by the redoubtable Mr Spinks (and allegedly built to enable the general manager of the London & Birmingham Railway, Captain Mark Huish, who came to live at Harlesden House in 1847, to have easy access to his office at Euston), Harlesden was on the map.

The 1851 census reveals that the population of Harlesden was 562, chiefly made up of farmers, farm labourers and railwaymen – served by the old inns like the *Crown* (recently closed) and the *Green Man*. In the 1860s, Harlesden's development began to gather speed. During this decade, row after row of streets was built, often by builders each with a few houses to erect, so that a coherent style rarely emerged. They housed railway workers, laundry workers and bakery staff. Some of the streets were named after local landowners – Colonel R.T. Nightingale-Tubbs gave his name to Tubbs and Nightingale Roads, while a mansion like Bramshill Lodge gave its name to the road alongside what is now the county court house.

Even so, until the 1870s, Harlesden still regarded itself as a rural community and thus found itself bitterly opposed to the idea of becoming part of a civic authority, which the citizens of the more urban area of Willesden, namely Kilburn, were struggling to achieve. The debate raged furiously for five years until, in 1875, the electors of the whole parish decided to obtain and were granted the local board, which then governed Willesden until the urban district council took over in 1895. George Furness, the leading Harlesden resident, ensconced in Roundwood House, having vigorously stood against local government, accepted defeat gracefully and became the first chairman of the new board. Amos Beeson (1859-1938) and his brothers ran a thriving ironmongers in the middle of Harlesden High Street (numbers 42-46) and a forge. In his 70s, Amos gave talks on his recollections of Harlesden in his youth and they are still a useful guide to the district of those days.

By the end of the century, Harlesden had now grown to about 10,000 people; the green, which once looked like a scene from a sleepy American Western main street, now resembled the busy urban thoroughfare with horse-drawn buses and a fine Jubilee Clock (erected for Queen Victoria's Golden Jubilee in 1887), with many excellent shops lining both sides of the road. There was All Souls' Church (1879), the public library (1894), a Methodist church rebuilt and enlarged in 1882 (and then bombed during the Second World War) and the court house in St Mary's Road (now rebuilt in Acton Lane). The Roman Catholic Church of Our Lady of Willesden in Nicoll Road was rather later, in 1931, replacing an earlier one in Crownhill Road.

The High Street was widened in 1906, to some shopkeepers' alarm, to allow the construction of a tramway, but this simply strengthened the success of this local centre. The growing population, wide-eyed and speechless, welcomed early cinemas with showings of silent films in St Mary's Hall and then in purpose built picture palaces such as the Coliseum and the Electric Palace. The Hippodrome – Willesden's (and Brent's) only theatre until the Tricycle came to Kilburn High Road in the 1980s – was opened triumphantly in 1907 and continued a flourishing career until, sadly, it was bombed in 1941 and never rebuilt. It was replaced later by offices. There was even the Harlesden Symphony Orchestra, formed in 1912, which later became first the Willesden and then the Brent Symphony Orchestra and is still merrily playing.

While the area round the original green developed into a series of housing estates, south of the railway was mainly industrial. An early and long-lasting company was McVitie & Price who, in 1902, sent the young Alexander Grant to set up their London factory on a greenfield site near Willesden Junction (handy for the link to Scotland – although their northern base was at Edinburgh). This created a base to which others followed – notably Heinz for many years, also in Waxlow Road.

The population continued to swell and, after the First World War, the local council (especially in the '30s and after, when the Labour Party took control) began building homes to meet the growing need. The Irish community was among the first to be attracted to the area. Then, after the famous *Empire Windrush* brought its West Indian migrants to Britain, Harlesden became a centre for Caribbean settlers and then for Hindus and Bangladeshis – a truly cosmopolitan town. A GP practising in Buckingham Road in the 1950s may have had dreams about his home land, but Dr Hastings Banda did indeed later return to Malawi to become its president, leaving behind a warm network of friendships. With the changing pattern of the population, so the religious observances supported the varied forms of prayer. Former churches and chapels became West Indian or Muslim places of worship. The variety reflected and represented the multi-ethnic and multi-cultural terrain that Brent had proudly become.

Queen's Park Estate (West Kilburn)

Separated by Kilburn Lane, an ancient field path from Watling Street to the Harrow Road, is the Queen's Park area of Paddington (now Westminster), also known as West Kilburn. It was part of the Malorees estate, belonging to All Souls' College – the northern half of which is in Willesden.

When the London & Birmingham Railway was built in 1837, it cut through several farms, leaving fields on both sides. Those fields down to the Grand Junction (now Union) canal remained largely untouched although, further south, as Kensal new town developed, some changes began – St John's Church was built in 1844.

It remained as fields until about 1874, when the wonderfully named Artizans', Labourers' and General Dwellings company, which had been formed some years earlier by William Austin to build decent houses for industrial working men, bought some 80 acres in this area between Kilburn Lane and the Harrow Road. It seems that they named it in honour of the Queen, and Queen's Park station, on the line out of Euston – opened following the Royal Agricultural Show of 1879 – was named from the estate. To the east, St Peter's Park, around Walterton Road, also began developing, but the new Queen's Park went ahead rapidly.

Roads going north-south were named First, Second, etc Avenue, and the cross roads were named alphabetically, although names rather than letters were soon added. For example there was Alperton Street, from the district in Wembley from whose brickworks materials were shipped along the canal, and Droop and Farrant Streets, after two of the company's directors.

The two-storeyed houses are well designed and attractively decorated with pediments, semi-circular arches and above all the monogram of the entwined initials of the company's name.

Queen's Park Rangers Football Club started here at Droop Street (later Queen's Park) School in 1882. Harrison Ainsworth, the famous novelist who lived at Kensal Manor House, walked down to St John's Church to act as churchwarden – and is remembered by Ainsworth House in Kilburn Lane. Charles Pinkham, who became closely involved in Willesden affairs, moved to Droop Street in 1881 and then to Kensal Rise, where he joined with Charles Langler in house building.

Among the many public buildings on the estate are St John's Church, the Congregational church (later URC), the library, Queen's Park Hall, which still remains within the building on the first floor, and several schools including Droop Street and the senior board school in Kilburn Lane (actually on Brent land), which later became the Moberley Youth Centre.

The Harrow Road through this part of London is not the most attractive of streets but is enlivened by the older and some newer buildings serving what remains a great community.

1 In 1879, the Royal Agricultural Society chose Kilburn for their annual touring show. They chose a literally greenfield site between the London & North-Western Railway and the North London Line, which crossed the southern half of Willesden. It was opened on 30 July by the Prince of Wales, with exhibits and visits by the Queen herself. It turned out to be the rainiest summer for years and 'Kilburn and mud became synonymous' was the terse summary in the *Illustrated London News*.

2 A parade of horses past the royal box at the Royal Agricultural Show, 1879.

3 Kilburn Lane was the long-established boundary between Willesden and Paddington (now Brent and Westminster). The name Queen's Park is associated with estates on both sides of the road. Much of the housing on the road was developed by the grandly named 'Artizans', Labourers' and General Dwellings Company' and their initials are seen intertwined over the doors of their houses. This picture, from about 1900, is looking west from Bravington Road.

4 Queen's Park in 1910. In the 1880s a campaign to use the old Royal Agricultural Show site as a 'People's Park' succeeded when the owners, the Ecclesiastical Commissioners, changed their minds and gave the land on condition that the Corporation of London made it into a place for the public to use. They had in mind that this generosity would pay off because of the development advantage that they would obtain for the surrounding area. The park was then laid out and opened on 5 November 1887 by the Lord Mayor of London, Sir Reginald Hanson – obviously and appropriately named in honour of Queen Victoria's Golden Jubilee.

5 No park would be complete without a bandstand – or a drinking fountain, as in the previous picture, in 1910. Concerts were held here regularly and during and after the Centenary celebrations in 1987, it has been used on the Open Day in September each year.

6 The park would not have been able to get the go-ahead without a benefaction from William Ward (1796-1881), whose generosity is recorded on his tombstone in the cemetery at St Matthew's Church, Brixton.

7   As this photo of Queen's Park from 1947 shows, the care for the oasis of greenery, comfort and neighbourliness has been kept up by the Corporation of London staff, working from their depot near Kingswood Avenue.

8   A typical greetings card from about 1906 comes from an era when telephones hardly existed and post collections and deliveries in London took place several times a day. Clockwise from the left: St John's Church at the corner of Kilburn Lane and Harrow Road; topiary in Queen's Park; the Congregational church in the Harrow Road, West Kilburn (Queen's Park); the bandstand in the park; and Harvist Road (now Kensal Rise) Primary School.

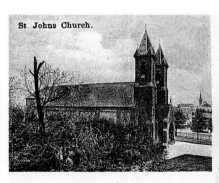

9   After Queen's Park opened, the Ecclesiastical Commissioners reaped their reward as the surrounding area became ripe for development. Kingswood Avenue borders the park on the east and the roads leading off towards Salusbury Road form a cluster, the origin of whose names is maddeningly unidentifiable. This 1961 picture reveals the start of the 'gentrification' of the estate, which today has cars on every available space.

10   During the First World War, over 360 of the many Belgian refugees came to Willesden, including a number of children. They were placed in homes in Brondesbury Park and nearby. A school in the Congregational church in Wrentham Avenue was set up in April 1916. They are seen here in 1916 enjoying the pleasure and safety of Queen's Park.

11   In the 1890s, a campaign was launched by the vigorous Dr J.C. Crone to take advantage of the Free Library Act and it succeeded when, within a few months of each other, three were opened. This one in Kilburn was the first (followed by Harlesden and Willesden Green). It was designed by Edmeston and Gabriel, with their delightful features of turret and oriel window, and was opened by the Rev J.F.C. Weldon, the Headmaster of Harrow School no less, on 30 January 1894.

12   This aerial view of Salusbury Road area in 1987 gives a good idea of the serried rows of late Victorian housing, built during a frenzy of development in the 1890s, when Willesden was the fastest-growing district in London – four houses a day being completed. Queen's Park Station is in the centre left and Brondesbury ridge in the distance.

13 This early photo (1890) shows the junction of Harvist Road and Salusbury Road – it looks a little like a scene from a Wild West movie. The Kilburn Police Station has since been completely rebuilt.

14 Twenty years later, this view up the length of Salusbury Road in about 1910 tells us a lot about the district. The 'Peeler' at the door of the police station comfortably surveys the peaceful scene: hand and horse-drawn carts are busy delivering goods; a lad is carrying a basket of bread loaves; the gas lamps reflect the work of Council Surveyor O.C. Robson's carefully planned work in street lighting and there is an air of purposefulness about Queen's Park in Edwardian England.

15   This view of Salusbury Road in 1910 gives a good picture of the shopping centre – little different from today in layout, except that the businesses will all be different and the gas light is now modern electric. The name comes from the family who acquired land in the area in the late 18th century and then sold it to the Ecclesiastical Commissioners.

16   The expanding district around Salusbury Road and Queen's Park was created as a new parish, St Anne's, in 1899 and the new church, designed by the brothers J.E. and J.P. Cutts, was dedicated in 1905. It lasted for 90 years and was then replaced by a very modern new building opened in 1998, which it shares with the congregation of St Andrew's United Reform Church. Its church hall and also a large part of Kilburn Grammar School next door were destroyed when a flying bomb landed in Paddington cemetery in June 1944. This illustration is from 1905.

17 St Anne's Church is on the right of this 1906 view of Salusbury Road, looking north, with Kilburn Grammar School further on, in 1908.

18 Williams the boot repairer at 32 Salusbury Road, a few doors from Queen's Park Station in about 1900; it may be Mr Williams in the doorway. This was typical of the small shops that still form the heart of the commercial part of the road, though there are probably more food premises now than 100 years ago.

19 The *Falcon* pub has become a landmark on the southern edge of Willesden, becoming the gateway to Queen's Park, seen in 1960. It was opened in the 1860s and, while it has seen its ups and downs (it is now on an island site surrounded by swirling traffic), it seems as popular as ever.

20 In 1978 Lady Mary Wilson, wife of the recent Prime Minister, Harold Wilson came to Aylestone School to read from the *Brent Anthology of Verse* a collection of poems written by students in the borough and talk about poetry with pupils from the school, along with the teacher Lyle Conquest.

21   At the northern end of Salusbury Road, Winchester Avenue was part of the late Victorian development stretching up towards Brondesbury. The series of streets was built with solid, terraced, two-storey, three-bedroomed town houses. At the corner, as seen in about 1900, is the shop owned by the then large grocery firm of W.H. Cullen. In the early 1960s, Willesden Council carried on the modernising of its older housing stock and part of this road was redeveloped with blocks of flats such as Mapes House.

22   You might say 'Spot the Difference' with this 1987 picture of the same corner.

23 This charming print engraved by J.R. Robbins of Paddington Cemetery (designed by Thomas Little) seen in its year of opening in 1855. The layout is of a horseshoe shape and intersecting paths cross at the two chapels. It was taken over by Westminster Council who later sold off several of its cemeteries for the princely sum of £1. Brent Council took it over and made it a welcoming open space, while protecting its status as a burial ground.

24 Kilburn Grammar School was opened in 1898 by Dr Bonavia Hunt, moving to Salusbury Road in 1900. The Bishop of London, Mandell Creighton, dedicated the new building and old boys call themselves 'Old Creightonians' in his memory. It continued to flourish as the principal boys' school in Willesden, until in 1967 it became part of the comprehensive system, later merged with the girls' school opposite and then succumbed to a falling school population and closed in 1987. It was then sold to a Muslim education foundation. This picture of Form V is from 1903 with the headmaster, Mr Evan Evans, on the left.

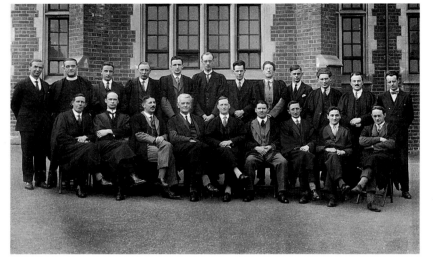

25 Kilburn Grammar staff in 1927. The head, Mr J. McLeish, is in the centre of the front row. The author can recall Williams, Yarwood and Gould (Latin) immediately behind the head; Bill Bentley (maths), second from left in front and 'Sammy' Burton (geography) third from right – other Old Creightonians may recall even more names.

26 This view of my old school, Kilburn Grammar, in 1908 just a few years after it opened in Salusbury Road, also shows the Willesden Council's electricity office just beyond it up the hill; newly planted trees will soften the hard edges of the street scene – what a shame that so many of them have been removed.

27 The Grand Cinema in 1913 in Lonsdale Road, off Salusbury Road, was one of the growing spate of 'cinematograph houses' in the years just before and after the First World War, which reflected the movie-going fashion. At its peak there were over 30 cinemas in Brent – now there are just two.

28 This street scene in 1900 of the council offices on the left with the fire station next to it (and the library beyond that) is a typical 1900 picture with a few people representing the many who would use the road each day. The offices were recently absorbed by a rebuilt police station, stretching from the corner to the library.

29 Willesden was an early convert to municipal electricity–but not for long. The council began to supply power in 1903 from its own generating station at Taylor's Lane but sold up in 1904 to a private company from which it bought back the energy – until the system was nationalised in 1947. However, it maintained its own offices for customers to pay their bills and this 1926 picture is of the office in Salusbury Road, next to Kilburn Grammar School – and to the sweet shop with liquorice wheels for one penny!

30 Opposite Kilburn Grammar School was the Maria Grey Training College for women teachers. It moved to Salusbury Road in 1892 when this sketch was made – it was then virtually country and the students used to talk of haymaking, daisy-gathering and the singing of the larks. It shared its premises with Brondesbury and Kilburn Girls' High School until the college moved to Twickenham in 1969.

31 The Brondesbury and Kilburn Girls' School at the top of Salusbury Road in 1900. It was a highly successful girls' school in Willesden. It merged with Kilburn Grammar in 1973 and eventually closed in 1987 due to falling school rolls and was sold by Brent Council, along with Kilburn Grammar, to a Muslim Education Trust.

32 Originally called Mortimer Road (the western part still bears the name), it was renamed Harvist Road from Edward Harvist, a successful brewer in 16th-century London who was imbued with the Elizabethan ethic of using his wealth to help others. He left money to repair roads in north-west London and also as a fund to help needy people and local good causes–as residents of Brent have found out over the years. This view in 1910 at the corner with Milman Road with a gate into the park would only differ from the scene today because of parked cars.

33 A picture of the dinner of the Willesden Council Officials' Club in 1904 – the men (of course, men only) are in their finery, sharing what we would call 'bonding together' over a satisfying meal.

34 This remarkable drawing by the architects Edmeston & Gabriel lovingly depicts the elaborate design for the block of council offices – remarkable even in 1894 for presenting the face of local government so completely and with such style and panache. The library remains, but the other buildings have been supplanted over the years by the police station's expanding needs.

35 Chevening Road in about 1910 as it would have looked to the younger John Beales. It was originally built, together with Harvist Road, as an approach road to the Royal Agricultural Show of 1879 by the Ecclesiastical Commissioners and developed after Queen's Park was opened for middle-class dwellings. This view towards Queen's Park shows horse-drawn vehicles – still the only means of transport–and also several of O.C. Robson's gas-lit street lamps.

36 A last look at Kilburn Grammar School Hall (known as the Creighton Hall), taken in 1991 before it was handed over to the Muslim Foundation – where it continues to be a successful school.

37   A small Jewish community grew in Brondesbury with master-builder Solomon Barnett at its head and, in 1905, he was able to lead them in the opening ceremony of the synagogue in Chevening Road, shown in this photograph from 1907. The principal guest was Sir Marcus Samuel (later Lord Bearsted) and the officiating minister was the Chief Rabbi Adler. After the Second World War it was attacked by right-wing extremists and that, together with a declining population, led to its closure. It was sold to Brent Council who used it as community centre and later the Muslim Education Foundation, who owned the neighbouring schools, bought it. Brondesbury and Kilburn Girls' School can be seen in the background.

38   The demolition of houses in Winchester Avenue in the early 1960s was part of Willesden Council's massive programme to deal with outdated houses and the desperate shortage of homes.

39 St Laurence Church in Chevening Road was opened in 1906 to meet
the still-expanding area of Queen's Park and Kensal Rise. This delightful
picture shows it in 1970, but it was soon to become a victim of a declining
congregation. It reunited with Christ Church in Willesden Lane and closed
in 1971. It was replaced by Brent Council with a block of flats, named after
the church.

40   At the turn of the last century, Willesden's education board (soon to be given greater powers by the 1902 Education Act) was busy meeting the rapidly growing demand for school places. Salusbury Road School was opened in 1902 when this picture was taken. The ivy-clad building to the right is the caretaker's house. It was designed by the council's architect, Mr G.E.T. Lawrence.

41   Inside Salusbury Road Elementary School in 1910 Hundreds of children, perhaps one thousand, crowd into the hall.

42 In 1916, a station porter keeps passengers up to date at Queen's Park Station.

43 Harvist Road in 1987 – on the left are council flats, replacing bomb-damaged buildings, while beyond on the left and right one can study different styles of early 20th-century houses.

KENSAL

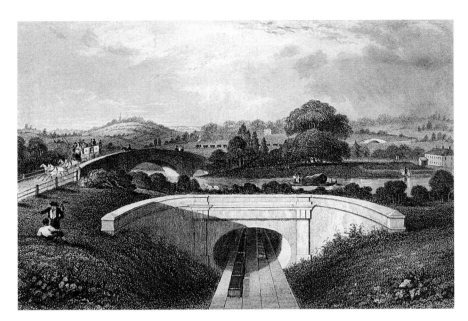

44   Robert Stephenson (son of George, who built the famous *Rocket*) was commissioned to build the first mainline railway in Britain – the London to Birmingham line, which opened its first section from Euston to Watford in 1837. Its route lay across southern Willesden, and then into Wembley. This lithograph shows the tunnel under the Harrow Road near the newly opened Kensal Green Cemetery.

45   All Souls' Avenue, *c.*1910, rising up from its junction with Wrottesley Road, is the heart of the estate formerly owned by All Souls' College Oxford. The lands in Willesden (and in Kingsbury) came to the college as a gift from Archbishop Thomas Chichele in 1443. The nearby roads bear the names of academics associated with the college, especially in the 19th century.

46 Dr John Smyth Crone was one of the outstanding personalities of the early days of Willesden District Council. Born in Belfast in 1858, he came to London, took his medical degree and by 1884 was in practice in Kensal Green. He was chairman several times and also served on Middlesex County Council. He was one of the stalwarts who obtained Willesden's free libraries, had a distinguished literary reputation and was particularly proud of his Irish heritage. He died in 1945.

47 Mr Hodgson's house in Chamberlayne Wood. He was a notable farmer in Willesden in the mid-19th century – he farmed in the area now Chapter Road – and was one of the first to succumb to the blandishments of developers.

48 St Martin's Church in Mortimer Road in 1910, is another Willesden church designed by the Cutts brothers. It was built on land allocated by All Souls' College and was originally intended to be a memorial to Dean Vaughan, a head of Harrow School, but later changed to the name it still uses.

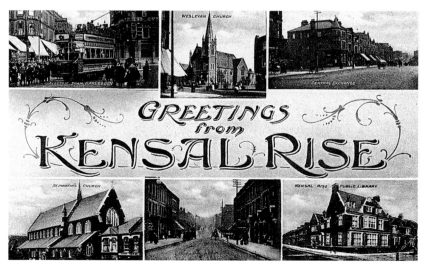

49 Another delightful greetings postcard, from about 1918, showing that this practice was not confined to seaside resorts. Clockwise from the left: not strictly Kensal Rise but High Street Harlesden, the tram driver, standing in the open, takes it round the corner by the *Royal Oak*; The Wesleyan Church, Chamberlayne Road (which was taken over by the Roman Catholic diocese and converted into the church of the Transfiguration in 1985); Central Exchange, part of Chamberlayne Road; Kensal Green Library in Bathurst Gardens; York Terrace, part of Acton Lane – another image which is not the Kensal Rise area; and St Martin's Church in Mortimer Road.

50 Harvist Road in about 1910 with one of the early motor buses going down to London stopping in a cloud of fumes outside the primary (elementary) school. It is no longer a bus route – a mixed blessing! In a few years it was the number six and routed down Kilburn Lane.

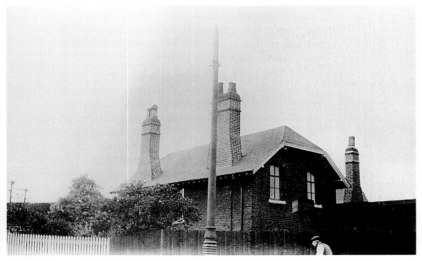

51 The North London Line was opened on 2 January 1860 from Camden Road to Old Oak Common, through Willesden Junction, linking up with an existing line to Kew. This is Kensal Green and Harlesden Station, open from 1861 to 1873. The stationmaster's house and booking office provided a station for visitors to Kensal Green Cemetery on Sundays. Honeypot railway bridge was on the right, leading to Green Lane, later Wrottesley Road. The station house remainder as a residence for railway staff for many years; it was pulled down after the Second World War.

52 Chamberlayne Road in 1939 – Kensal Rise Station is just visible behind the bus at its terminus; there is a Co-op shop on the left and a variety of other shops on the right coming down from the railway bridge and along to Harvist Road.

53 Okehampton Road at its junction with Chamberlayne Road in 1938, with the railings of Chamberlayne School on the right. I like the style of the roof and turret on the corner building.

54 By 1964, yellow lines are all over the main roads in Willesden; the van is turning out of Clifford Gardens. Chamberlayne Road School is in the distance on the right.

55 By the corner of Dagmar Gardens off Station Road in 1964, a Wonderloaf van is ready to deliver its load to – where else? – Breadways shop. Kensal Government Surplus Store was sill able to sell such goods twenty years after the end of the war.

56 Political parties like to have their own centres where possible. The Conservatives set up the Constitutional Club in Kensal Rise, at first in a house at 119 Chamberlayne Road (the Liberal Central Club was at 101) and then in a purpose-built headquarters (shown on the right), opened in 1927 at the corner of Hardinge Road. It was designed by George Sexton and his son, who were architects for many of Willesden's notable buildings. It was presumably not Empire Day, so a flag is not flying on the pole on this day in 1939. Its hall is named Pinkham Hall (See illustration 104).

57 Milk used to be sold from many small dairies (before most succumbed to competition from the giants such as Express, United and the Co-op). Welfords in Chamberlayne Road in 1924 was one of the larger dairies, with its own farm and bottling plant in Harlesden and at least 20 shops in Willesden and the vicinity.

58 Kempe Road *c.*1910 (named after a 19th-century prebendary of St Paul's Cathedral) is part of the estate on the western side of Queen's Park. Many of the houses were built by Charles Langler (hence the road named after him on the other side of Chamberlayne Road) and his partner Charles Pinkham (illustration 104).

59　Kensal Rise Station on the North London Line. In the furore about Willesden becoming a local board, in the 1870s, such was the intransigence of the country dwellers in Harlesden and Kensal Green that it made the urban residents of Kilburn consider hiving off from the rest of the parish, with the North London Line as their northern boundary – but it did not happen, of course. Here is a typical morning scene in April 1960.

60　After the three original libraries were built in Willesden, Kensal Rise sought to follow, but the money was only sufficient for a reading room at first. Nonetheless, the committee secured Mark Twain, the famous novelist and essayist who was visiting London at the time and staying at Dollis Hill House, to open it. On 27 September 1900 this was what he proudly carried out. A few weeks earlier he had been invited to the opening of the Central Line ('The Twopenny Tube') in June.

61 & 62 A few years later, in 1904, with the help of money from the Andrew Carnegie Trust, a lending library was added and here it is shown above, in 1910, with gates and lanterns, welcoming discerning readers to borrow their books. The picture below shows how it looked in 1928.

63 Empire Day celebrations in a class at Chamberlayne Wood School on 24 May 1920. It has been replaced by Commonwealth Day – 13 March – but it has scarcely the same ring to it.

64 An early class at Chamberlayne Wood School, which was opened in 1904, in the standard three-storey brick-built style, with separate entrances for infants and for junior boys and girls.

65 Wrentham Avenue was originally named Ladysmith Road, thus dating it to the Boer War siege at that town in September 1900. After the Crossman trunk murder and suicide in 1904 it was changed–not to Trunksville Road as suggested–but to its present name. This view, from 1910, at the corner of Crediton Road, gives a good view of the spire of the Wesleyan Methodist church in Chamberlayne Road, which later was reconsecrated as the Catholic Church of the Annunciation.

66 In 1963 the same road is flush with street trees and parked cars. This view is also looking towards Chamberlayne Road.

67 College Road School was set up in 1915 for children with what today would be called special educational needs. It was used until 1961 (the picture dates from just before its closure) and the site was then taken over for use by Brent as an education training and youth centre. More recently it has been rebuilt as the new Doyle nursery.

68 Prominent at the corner of Harvist and Chamberlayne Roads was the Harvist Road Elementary School (now Kensal Rise Primary), opened on 29 August 1898 – one of the earliest in Willesden after Acton Lane, which was the board's first. This picture, taken soon after the opening, is of 'people watching children doing something in the playground', as the official caption reads.

69 Going home from school – Harvist Road in about 1906. The cart on the extreme right seems to be selling vegetables – today it would be ice cream.

70 The grandly named National Athletic Ground seen on this 1895 map in the area north of the North London Line at Kensal Rise never became the success that was hoped for. In 1890 it was open and used by Queens Park Rangers as one of their many early grounds. It was reduced in size when Clifford Gardens was built and lost totally to the developers a few years later. There do not seem to be any photographs of this historic ground.

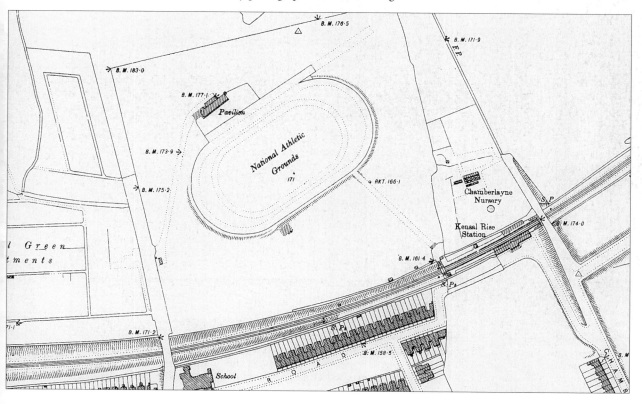

71 All Souls' College started to review their land holdings in this part of Willesden at about the time the Ecclesiastical Commissioners began their expansion nearer to Queen's Park. They sold a large acreage to the United Land Company, who were very active developers in this part of London. Purves was the land agent (and Hazel the solicitor) – hence Hazel Road and Purves Road, built around 1900 by Edward Vigers and other local builders and seen here in 1962.

72 Langler and Pinkham employed a local craftsman skilled in the practice of decorating the fascias of houses with stucco patterns known as pargeting. This is number 52 Clifford Gardens, with the owner Mrs Studman at her gate. The road was built in 1896 across the National Athletic Ground.

73 Willesden was badly hit during the Second World War by German air raids aimed at Willesden Junction, for obvious reasons. In 1947 the bomb site (caused by a flying bomb on 21 August 1944, where 20 people were killed) is pictured at the corner of College, Hazel and Mortimer Roads. It was later rebuilt with Kensal Rise Senior Club and council houses.

74 Victor Road in 1900 – it and Napier Road form a little enclave off the Harrow Road, although part of the large-scale development of Kensal Green. They are named after a long-forgotten war hero, Lord Robert Napier (1810-90), who was victorious at the battle of Magdala in Ethiopia in 1868. Apparently it was originally to be called Beaconsfield Road, which would have been a more recognisable name.

75   This photograph from the *Willesden Chronicle* of 1946 celebrates the golden wedding of Mr John and Mrs Rosetta Beales of Chevening Road. He was the owner of Alexander's Stores, a well-known furnishing store in Kilburn High Road, which operated for about 80 years until its closure in 1962. John Beales was its boss for much of that period until his retirement.

76   William Harrison Ainsworth (1805-82) came from Manchester to Kilburn in 1824 and began writing best-selling novels. In his day he was as popular as Charles Dickens, one of his friends. After his marriage he moved first to Kensal Lodge at 725 Harrow Road, where he frequently entertained other literary friends such as Thackeray and John Forster. Many of his books included references to his adopted home in Willesden. Kensal Lodge became Dr J.C. Crone's surgery and was eventually redeveloped as modern housing. He later moved next door to Kensal Manor House. This picture is from about 1930.

77   Kensal Manor House, *c.*1890. Although Ainsworth's later home at 733 Harrow Road was graced with the name 'manor house', it was never actually used as the name suggests. Later it was used as the office of a lively little local newspaper, the *Willesden Citizen*. It more recently became a scaffolding firm. Ainsworth is buried in Kensal Green Cemetery – of course.

78 At 784 Harrow Road, 4 Morris Place, near the corner with Warfield Road, is Mr Alfred Levi and his greengrocer's shop in 1910 (although *Kelly's Directory* lists this as a coal merchant).

79 The last horse-drawn tram from Paddington Green to Harlesden, near its depot in Trenmar Gardens College Park, with its splendid conductor and driver in his bowler hat. The service ran from 1886 to 1906 (the date of this picture) when electric trams, which began on the same route in December 1906, supplanted it.

80 The *Masons' Arms* in the Harrow Road, opposite Kensal Green Station, opened in the 1870s, and took its name from its proximity to the cemetery, thus celebrating the tombstone craftsmen. It has the last remaining cast-iron horse trough in Willesden.

81 This stretch of the long Harrow Road between Ravensworth and Victor Roads is part of a sequence of useful local shops that were then opposite Kensal Manor House. Here, in 1910, is Coates the grocer, as their sunblind clearly states, Victor Stores, from the neighbouring road, and a pawnbroker, an undertaker (Nodes) and others.

82   The *William IV* pub, *c.*1910 – its name dates it – built about the time of the opening of the cemetery in 1833 to serve the cemetery workers, many of whom lived nearby along the Harrow Road. Edward Warfield, who was the publican from 1895-1901, extended the site and the road next to the inn now bears his name. It recently upgraded itself and is once again a very popular hostelry. On the wall is painted an advert for Noakes & Co's fine ales.

83   Children at the gate to Princess Frederica School, in Purves Road, in 1900–the year its founder Emily Ayekbown sadly died. Sister Emily (born 1831) founded the Church Extension Association, which set up eight schools linked to the Church of England. These included, in Willesden, Gordon Memorial (long closed) and Keble Memorial in Crownhill Road. It was opened in 1889 by Princess Frederica of Hanover, a cousin of Queen Victoria, who was a patron of the association.

84 Harvist Road, near Queen's Park Station, in about 1899, with the park in the distance and the attractive 'butch gable' roof line of the housing, which is still in use.

85 The *Plough* on Harrow Road in 1804, on the corner with Ladbroke Grove, is actually on the other side of the road from Willesden, but its fame as one of the main inns on this highway deserves a mention. It is seen in this print of 1802. It was swept away in the 1990s with the widening of the Ladbroke Grove junction. It is often confused with the *Old Plough* in Regent Street off Kilburn Lane, now renamed *Paradise by Way of Kensal Green*.

86 The Turnpike Gate and House is depicted in this watercolour, by Amos Beeson, near Kensal Manor House about 1870–just before it was demolished as these trusts ended in 1872. Through the 18th and early 19th centuries the need to improve and maintain the main roads was recognised through the setting up of Turnpike Trusts empowered to levy tolls on vehicles, horses and even farm animals. The dues collected were used to maintain the roads.

BRONDESBURY

87 A typical part of Brondesbury Park (laid down in 1892), from the corner with Alverstone Road, pictured about 1910. Telephone wires are all carried on poles, street trees are newly planted.

88 Willesden parish, centred on St Mary's Church, grew slowly over hundreds of years. Then, as the expansion began in the 1850s, the growing population demanded its place of worship to be nearer to where they lived. The first daughter church was Christ Church on Willesden Lane. The site was chosen by Dr Charles W. Williams and work commenced in 1865. The building was completed and consecrated by the Bishop of London's representative on 21 November 1866. Its striking spire is a landmark, as this picture shows in 1895.

89 This charming painting of Christ Church by W. Juker was one of a series he did of local scenes in 1890. This one has a delightful touch of a man struggling with his umbrella in the wind.

FARADAY WEEK IN WILLESDEN

SOME REMARKABLE FLOOD-LIGHT PICTURES

We give below three striking photographs by Mr. J. W. Debenham, 182, Round-wood Road, Willesden, of the flood lighting of prominent local buildings

CHRIST CHURCH, BRONDESBURY, whose history is described in an article elsewhere in this issue

90 Faraday Week was celebrated in Willesden in February 1931, as shown in this press cutting from the *Willesden Chronicle*, by floodlighting Christ Church. This was the centenary of Faraday's great discovery that led to the development of electric power.

91   The Avenue, *c.*1902, was one of the grander streets in Victorian Willesden. Why do we no longer have drinking fountains at the street corners, even if there is a policeman on watch while the lad with the handcart takes a drink?

92   Willesden, especially Brondesbury, was highly sought after in mid-Victorian times. Its clean air, slight elevation and country aspect encouraged developers to meet a need for good-quality housing. Brondesbury Park (in 1910) was built with houses of a high standard, whose quality is maintained today, despite some dominating flats having replaced some of the attractive villas.

93 Willesden Lane in about 1910, looking up towards Christ Church. Among the grand houses on the left was number 163, which was used in the 1960s as Willesden Education Department offices and then as a special school, Vernon House.

94   The Church of England was much involved in education over many years; under the direction of the local church Christchurch School was set up in the 1890s in Willesden Lane. This mixed class with its teachers is from the 1920s.

95   The group of refugee Belgian children went to the King Albert School set up in the Congregational church, Wrentham Avenue (at the corner with Tiverton Road). A series of photographs shows them in school, in Queen's Park and at church. Here they are outside the church in 1916. They stayed until March 1919 before returning home.

96 The Mission House in Brondesbury Park. A grand edifice, seen in 1916, and one of the locations used by the Belgian refugee children.

97 Brondesbury Park Bowls Club–pictured is the pavilion in 1925–was located a little way from the district, as it is in Chatsworth Road by the corner of Mapesbury Road. The author used to stand on the railway bridge and watch the bowlers on the green.

98 One of the large architect-designed mansions, 'Rosedene', c.1900, in Christchurch Avenue, which was, infuriatingly to some, demolished to make way for council housing bearing the same name.

99 In October 1961, a common enough petty crime took place in Brondesbury Park by the junction with Sidmouth Road when a Middlesex County Council taxi carrying wages was ambushed and thieves stole £6,000. (They left £1,000 behind.)

100 St Monica's Home Hospital in 1900 in Brondesbury Park. It was a form of hospice, later absorbed into Willesden General Hospital.

101 The parish hall of Christ Church was built in 1929 in the grounds of the former Mapesbury House and was called, naturally, Mapesbury Hall. In 1959 it was taken over by Willesden Council and renamed the Majestic Rooms. It is still (though now privately run) an excellent venue for a wedding or similar function.

102 Brondesbury Manor House had a long history as one of the grander mansions standing in its own large grounds, landscaped in the 18th century by Humphry Repton. In 1880, it became a girls' boarding school and its later headmistress Lucy Soulsby wrote about it in her book, from which these two pictures are taken. This is the library. The school closed in 1934 (when it moved to the country) and was another one of the examples of local development vandalism when it was demolished to make way for a high-class estate, Manor House Drive.

103 The garden at Brondesbury Manor House during its use as a school. Miss Soulsby ran the school for many years in discreet privacy for the girls and on strictly Christian lines. Several girls were educated here who later became Conservative MPs.

104 Sir Charles Pinkham was undoubtedly one of the dominant figures of Willesden politics in his time. A Devonian, born in 1853, he came to London to Droop Street on the new Queen's Park estate, and then moved to Hazel Road. He set up a partnership with Charles Langler to build in Kensal Rise, as earlier pictures record. He was five times chairman of the Willesden UDC, a member of the county council, MP for West Middlesex and was responsible for securing Gladstone Park for the community. He died in March 1938 and is publicly recorded by the name Pinkham Way on a stretch of the North Circular Road.

105 Malorees School in Christchurch Avenue takes its name from the ancient estate in this area. It was one of the post-Second World War generation of junior and infant schools, built to cope with the post-war 'bulge', seen here in 1960.

HARLESDEN

106 The country village green–the *Royal Oak* in Harlesden High Street about 1878 and the *Green Man* just beyond. The *Royal Oak* had a garden at the back. It is now the only one of the old pubs left.

107 This unusual view, from about 1901, of the Jubilee Clock and the High Street looking east to the *Royal Oak* shows the street halfway between a village and a town as the next picture amply shows.

108 1907. Some shops are being pulled down in the High Street to make way for the new electric trams, due to run in 1908.

109 The centre of Harlesden about 1911. The Jubilee Clock was erected in 1887 and paid for by local residents. A number 18 bus is on its way to Willesden bus garage on this typical day, while pedestrians carefully avoid the tram lines.

110 Outside 150 High Street Harlesden, Mr Ernest James Gerres, baker and confectioner, proudly sits on his delivery cart. This picture is from 1904.

111 Pictured from the *Royal Oak*, Harlesden High Street in about 1910 looks busy and purposeful; on the right two sailors stand near the underground toilets. (Where have they gone to today?) On the left, Strange & Chitham the outfitters carried on until population changes called for a different range of shops.

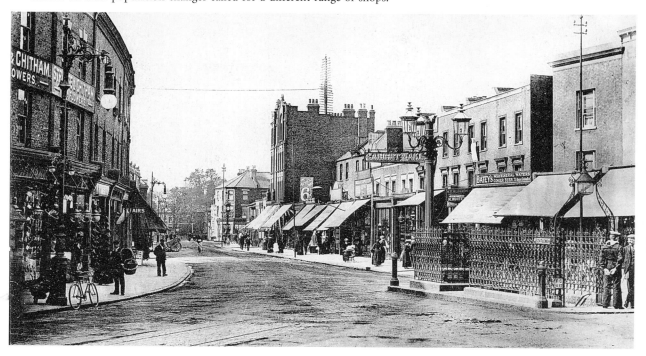

112 The Wesleyan Methodist church in 1900. It dominated the High Street for many years but was destroyed in the Second World War. Its modern replacement is still a landmark in the street.

113 A mass of overhead tram wires almost obscures The Cabin, at the corner of the High Street next to the Jubilee Clock. It was part of number 52, Mr Gregory's dairy, added on to the side of his building as if with glue.

114 The police station in Craven Park Road at the corner of St Mary's Road, about 1907. The bank on the other corner is still operating, under its later name. Behind the shops are the rarely noticed flats, which were part of the original development.

115 The new Harlesden Police Station, a little distance away from its predecessor, 1975.

116 Long since pulled down, this cabman's shelter in Craven Park Road was well used in about 1902, at a time when public transport had hardly started to function.

117 Harlesden Library was the second of the three original libraries in Willesden. Beaten by a few weeks by Kilburn, it was opened by Sir Henry Roscoe MP on 14 February 1894 with a stock of 6,400 books. The picture was taken soon after opening.

118 The refreshment pavilion in Roundwood Park, *c*.1900. Admire the ladies' hats and ponder to whom the postman is about to deliver his letters–or is he just stopping for a cup of tea?

119 Roundwood Park, 1900. Willesden Board bought Hunger Fields behind George Furness's Roundwood House in 1892 for £15,000. O.C. Robson, Willesden's superb engineer, converted the land, at a cost of another £11,000, into 'a Garden of Eden without the snakes'. It was opened on 11 May 1895 and 'dedicated for ever to the people' – a promise that has been kept over the years.

120 Over the years Roundwood Park has seen many festive activities. Here Dr J.C. Crone (from illustration number 46) has set out his garden party in 1900 with this lovely group of well-dressed men and women.

121 By the water fountain in the park, below the bandstand, a group of men are meeting in true Edwardian dress, though the reason for their meeting is not known to us.

122 Leghorn Road, *c.*1910, was one of the thoroughfares off Wrottesley Road that bears a name associated with George Furness's engineering achievements in Italy and in the Crimea in the mid-19th century, before he settled down to become the First Gentleman of Willesden.

123 Acton Lane in 1917, with a view of the Baptist church, which lost the top of the spire during the Second World War. The church was built on the site of Harlesden House, one of the original big houses in the district.

BRAMSHILL
ROAD. N.W.

124 Harlesden old Manor House, probably about 1870. It may be called a 'manor house' but it is more like the country farm house it really was. Note the peculiarly tall chimney. In the field was a pond where it is said a man drowned his wife after a quarrel. Manor Park Road was driven right through the farm.

125 This is Manor Park Road *c.*1900. The large house on the corner is named 'Fairholme'.

126 Willesden's newly formed Poor Law district swiftly moved in 1896 to set up their own workhouse – this and the Infirmary were opened in Acton Lane in 1903 with places for 150 sick and 250 in the workhouse. It is now the remaining middle section of Central Middlesex Hospital.

127 Amos Beeson (1859-1938) was part of a well-known family in Harlesden. They ran the smithy at 42 to 46 High Street and also in the Croft. Amos was a master wheelwright and, with his brother Charles, set up the volunteer fire brigade in 1881. He gave lectures on the history of Harlesden, with some of his own paintings as illustrations.

128 (opposite)   Knowles Tower, *c.*1910, was an unusual building in rural Harlesden with its tall chimneys, near to Roundwood House and to Hunger Hill Common Field, which later became Roundwood Park. It was used by the Inland Revenue for a period during the First World War. It was bought by the council and pulled down in 1937 to become part of Roundwood Park.

129 James Wright was part of a well-known family in this part of Willesden. He farmed here and was also clerk to the Bloomsbury County Court in mid-Victorian London. His land stretched from today's Park Parade (then part of Harlesden Road) to Keble School to the north. His house is seen here in 1870.

130 Willesden Cottage Hospital from its beginning in 1893 constantly had to raise money. A carnival was one good way and this one, in 1900 on Shoolbred's nearby ground, was very successful. (Shoolbred was a well-known furniture store in Tottenham Court Road and provided this sports ground for its staff.)

131 The 1908 Olympics in London included the Marathon, run from Windsor to the White City Stadium – establishing the modern distance for the race. Dorando Pietri of Italy is seen passing the Jubilee Clock – he was in the lead. When he reached the stadium, he was the first to cross the finishing line. Then tragedy prevented him being accorded the accolade. He was so fatigued by the time he reached the White City that he started running round the wrong way; officials helped, and half-carried him across the finishing line. Thus, even though he was the first, he was, sadly, disqualified and the race was awarded to the second to finish, Johnny Hayes of the USA.

132 A solitary cart stands in Harlesden Green in 1877, with Webster's saddlery on the left. It retains the look of a little village high street, before all begins to change.

133 Willesden's only permanent theatre, the Hippodrome in Harlesden High Street, seen here in 1911, was built by the great theatre architect Frank Matcham. It opened in September 1907, was bombed in October 1940 and never reopened. Many of the musical hall stars of that time appeared here, Marie Lloyd, George Robey, Lucan and McShane (who lived for a while in Forty Lane Wembley) among them.

134 Arthur Guinness & Co. had brewed their stout in Dublin for many years. In the 1930s they decided to establish a brewery in Britain and decided on Park Royal. A superb brick building designed by Sir Giles Gilbert Scott was opened in 1934. Recently, the firm decided to withdraw from brewing in England and their estate is being redeveloped. The building will not be preserved.

135 At the Odeon Cinema in Harlesden on 11 June 1955, a tinfoil collection is made on behalf of guide dogs for the blind. In the past year, local members had collected nearly 600lbs of tinfoil. Built by Oscar Deutsch, the exciting chain of art deco cinemas was no better at resisting television and other entertainments in the 1960s and, after it was pulled down, a block of flats, Odeon Court, recalls its past glories.

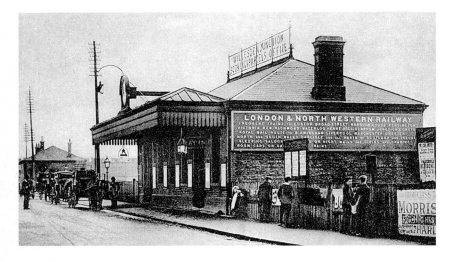

136 Willesden Junction Station in 1891, when the new booking office was opened. Taxis wait for passengers at this busy, vast station. The novelist Anthony Trollope complained that he got lost and it was said that the ghosts of passengers who died before they could get out haunted it!

137 Sellon's Farm in 1870 lies in what is still the bend of Harlesden Road (by the junction with Wrottesley Road), and Sellons Avenue and Springwell Avenue now recall it. John Baker Sellons was a magistrate who was one of the Willesden Enclosure Commissioners in 1815; his farm was later owned by John Wright – here it is weather-boarded and ivy-clad – and has long since been demolished for housing.

138 The Constitutional Hall in St Mary's Road in about 1908 where, among other activities, film shows were given as early as 1902 and by 1908 there were regular programmes twice nightly. However, by 1914 it had become a labour exchange. On the left is the magistrates' court building, built in 1892. It was replaced in the 1980s by new building in Church End.

139 Nicoll Road was one of the early changes when Harlesden went from country to town. This scene is from 1900. The name comes from one of Willesden's older families who were among the beneficiaries of the 1815 Enclosure Act.

140 Manor Park Road was cut through the old farm after the manor house was demolished about 1880. In the 1960s, around the time this picture was taken, the Coliseum, which had started as a cinema in 1912, remained popular until the general decline in cinema-going. It is still in use for entertainment of a different kind – and note the Salvation Army citadel next door!

141 Station Road in 1900. One of the GPO (Royal Mail) sorting office buildings is dated 1887 and its neighbour bears the initials of Edward VII–the early recognition of the NW10 post office. Other buildings have changed and these street trees have gone, but the service continues.

142 Welford's Dairy at Haycroft Farm where, in about 1900, haymaking is in full swing. It was one of the larger independent dairies in Willesden and set up a number of its own dairy shops.

143 McVitie & Price (*c*.1910) opened their biscuit factory in Waxlow Road in the early part of the last century and were soon employing some 500 local workers – producing a greater output than their parent at Edinburgh – and still producing 'better biscuits' today.

144 The fascination for posting bills on the fence in Acton Lane in 1905 remains a mystery to the author, but thirty years later it is still going on – see next picture.

145 Acton Lane in 1935, near Connaught Road.

146 Like many large houses, the entrance to Roundwood House was protected by its lodge, seen here in the distance along Harlesden Road about 1895.

147 Ploughing in May 1931 in Harlesden Road (Roundwood Paddocks) near the hospital, before the town swept over the fields here.

148 A Catholic chapel was built in Manor Park Road in 1886 and given up when the Church of Our Lady was built in Crownhill Road in 1907, next to the Convent of Jesus and Mary. Our Lady of Willesden in Nicoll Road in turn superseded this in 1931.

149 In 1888 the Convent of Jesus and Mary School was opened in Crownhill Road and has continued to expand and flourish ever since. It absorbed the site of the church next door and has Keble Memorial C of E School as a neighbour.

150 Harlesden House was leased by Robert Tubbs in 1847 to Captain Mark Huish, the general manager of the London & Birmingham Railway, so it was convenient for him to travel to his office from Harlesden Station to Euston. Tubbs owned much of Harlesden through the Enclosure Act. (Tubbs Road is named after him.)

151 Outside the *Royal Oak* in the High Street the horse tram reaches its terminus in Harlesden before returning to Paddington (Lock Bridge, near Amberley Road). In a couple of years' time the horse will be put out to graze as electric power takes over.

152 'Our Brave Firemen' – a worthy tribute to the volunteer brigade in Harlesden in 1904, a few years after receiving the horse-powered appliance. It was kept at the back of Beeson's Yard in the High Street.

153 The Grand Man of Willesden: George Furness. Born in Longstone, Derbyshire in 1820, he built up a large civil engineering business with contracts in Italy and in the Crimea after the war there. On settling back in Harlesden he became involved in building the drainage system under the Thames Embankment. He became the first chairman of the Willesden Local Board and died, unspoiled by his wealth, at Roundwood House in 1906.

154 F.A. Wood (1822-1904), who worked for the family grocery firm but whose main gift to his adopted home of Willesden was compiling the most detailed history of the parish, much of which he hand-wrote. He found time to play an active part in local politics and followed George Furness as chairman of the board from 1881 to 1888.

155 O. Claude Robson (1849-1924). Highly praised by F.A. Wood when he joined, Robson worked for Willesden Council for 43 years as surveyor and engineer, making roads, lighting them first with gas and then electricity, creating parks, especially Roundwood Park, and doing almost everything else that physically underpins a well-run authority.

156 In July 1959, the Queen Mother made one of her regular visits to a London Borough. Looking young and radiant for her 59 years, she is doing just what she did when the author as Mayor greeted her some years later – appraising local gardens.

157 Willesden's Carnival (this is the 1949 one) was the highlight of the summer – floats carried displays and the Carnival Queen, Miss Grace Vail; Roundwood Park was alive with fun and jollity and thousands crowded round the stalls and in the funfair.

158 The Mayor, Sam Viant MP, looks on as the new open-air theatre is launched in Roundwood Park in 1960. Planned by the Entertainments Manager 'Bomber' Harris it was part of the successful campaign to make the parks and libraries available to people to use.

159 On a serious note, in May 1977 the *Willesden Chronicle* reported that 'as police closed in on a Provisional IRA terror squad responsible for a series of bombings in London, a young nurse fled the country leaving an arsenal under the bed' at 89 Wrottesley Road.

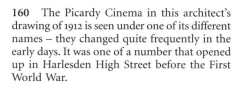
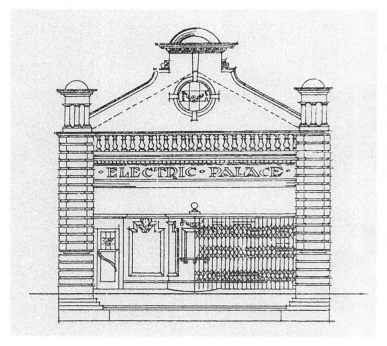

160 The Picardy Cinema in this architect's drawing of 1912 is seen under one of its different names – they changed quite frequently in the early days. It was one of a number that opened up in Harlesden High Street before the First World War.

161 The Coliseum Cinema in Manor Park Road, opened in 1912, was perhaps the best of the group that nestled around the *Royal Oak* area but, like all of them, it gave way to trends and became a pub and a club.

162 The tram service from Acton to Willesden Green and beyond crossed in Craven Park with the route from Paddington to Wembley; it is seen here in about 1912 outside the original Harlesden Police Station.

163 (above)   Willesden Cottage Hospital in Harlesden Road was opened in 1893 after a great local fundraising effort and with the help of the benefactor Passmore Edwards. It began with eight beds and gradually expanded to about 140. It is now a Health and Care centre within the NHS.

164 (top right)   Roundwood House, pictured in 1903, dates from the early 19th century and was bought by George Furness in 1856 from a relation of Lord Cardigan, of the Charge of the Light Brigade. His son, George J., who was MP for West Willesden and chairman of Willesden Hospital, continued to occupy it. It was sold to the council in 1937, pulled down and the land added to Roundwood Park. Some was used for a youth centre and an old people's home.

165 (right)   The *Royal Oak* in Harlesden High Street, as an electric tram turns the corner. Other activities – a horse and cart, shoppers, cyclists – depict a typical day in about 1911.

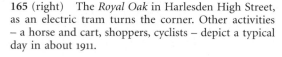

166   The opening of the extension to Willesden County School by Lord Burnham in May 1932. (This was the author's wife's old school.) The speaker is in the centre; on his left is the head, Mr Wallis, and on his right Dr Evan Davies, the education officer for Willesden District Council. In the late 1990s it was pulled down and replaced by Capital City Academy.

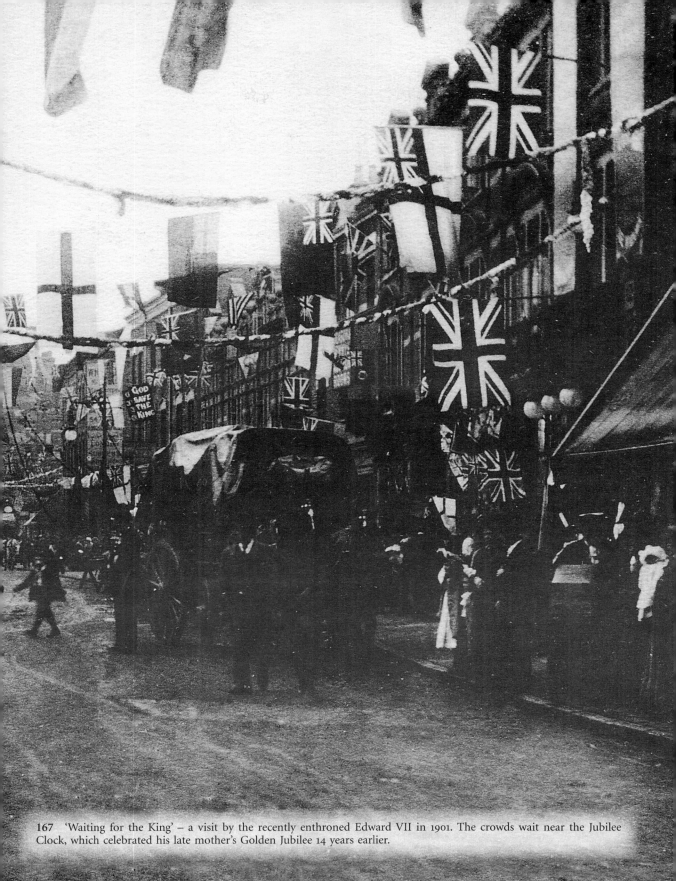

167 'Waiting for the King' – a visit by the recently enthroned Edward VII in 1901. The crowds wait near the Jubilee Clock, which celebrated his late mother's Golden Jubilee 14 years earlier.

168 & 169   A contrast – Harlesden High Street in 1902 and in 1980.

170   Along the eastern part of the High Street were a number of small detached villas. This is Zion House, opposite Nightingale Road, occupied in 1877 by Mr John Roberts.

171 An amazing find among old cuttings led the author to this monument in Willesden New Cemetery, created from Devon granite, of 'Schwarz of the Kalahari'. Professor Ernest Schwarz, born in London in 1880, became a famous geologist and led expeditions to the Kalahari, successfully bringing water to the desert. He died of fever in 1928 and his wife decided on this striking memorial in his home town.

172 Harlesden Road around 1902, now called Park Parade. On the right is the junction with Rucklidge Avenue. At the corner, hidden by the trees, is the Willows, a charming villa, recalled by houses on Willow Terrace, and beyond it is the Friends' Meeting House. However, at the far end of Rucklidge Avenue, numbers 154 and 156, there was, for a few years at the very end of the 19th century, the Royal Hygienic Hospital, set up by Dr Thomas Allinson (1858-1918). It was a nursing home based on the values of 'natural living' as he described his philosophy. On more practical lines, he developed a form of wholemeal bread, which is still on sale today.

173 The London County Council bought some land across the border of Kilburn Lane to open their higher grade board school in 1885. This marvellous picture of the assembly in 1900, complete with string orchestra, emulates the public school morning prayers—some 500 boys packed in here. After the hymn, prayers would be led by the headmaster and then they would go off to their studies. The school later became the Moberly Youth Centre.

174 St John the Evangelist Church, at the corner of Kilburn Lane and Harrow Road, was almost the first substantial building here. Built by H.E. Kendall and opened in 1844 it stands out on the main road – a major landmark. It is also opposite to Ladbroke Grove coming up from the south. It is seen here in about 1875.

175 Farrant Street in 1908, which is no longer on the map as it was part of the redevelopment of parts of the estate by Westminster Council. The original houses along the Harrow Road frontage from St John's Church eastwards were the largest section of the rebuilding, while some other areas became open spaces.

176 Queen's Park Public Library was opened in 1890 under the Chelsea Vestry, since this area was, curiously and historically, a detached part of the Chelsea parish until 1900. It was designed by Karslake and Mortimer and built for £2,573 15s. It was and remains a great success. The reading room in the library, photographed in 1936, offered the residents of the estate and of Kensal town the opportunity not only to borrow books but to read the newspapers and keep up-to-date with the world.

177 Queen's Park Hall, seen here in 1911, at the corner of First Avenue was planned by the Artizans' Company – with their full name emblazoned above the ground floor – to serve the community as a public hall and as a working men's literary institute. It was very successful, with band concerts, arts exhibitions and so on, and it remains today as a boxing gym and youth club, though the shops on the ground floor are empty.

178 Queen's Park Congregational Church in *c.*1900. It was preceded by a hall until the permanent edifice was opened in June 1890 and proved very popular with its congregation. It became a URC church when the Congregational and Presbyterian Churches merged in 1972; it was considered for rebuilding but this has not yet happened.

179 Kilburn Lane about 1902, near Bravington Road and not far from the *Falcon* pub. This was a lively little shopping centre serving the northern part of the Queen's Park estate, built by the United Land Company. The shops have of course changed, but the names are a reminder of the importance of the local shopkeeper.

180 Alperton Street in 1910 was one of the 'alphabetically named' streets. It refers to the brickworks run by Henry Haynes in Alperton in Wembley and serving the Artizans' Company with their bricks and tiles delivered by canal barge.

181 Droop Street was named after one of the directors of the company and gives a view of the paced streets and the rows of chimney pots from a photograph of 1963.

182 Droop Street School was opened in 1877. A few years later it became the home of QPR, when some old boys formed a football team, which merged with another local club. They played at first at different grounds, including Kensal Rise and Kilburn, before eventually settling at Loftus Road. It is seen here c.1910.

183 An 1865 OS map of the district showing the close-knit street pattern.

184 ALGDC maintenance staff in 1955 – still providing a service after 80 years.

185 Fourth Avenue was one of the numbered avenues running north-south, apparently in imitation of the practice in Washington DC, the capital of the USA. The entrance to the Queen's Park Library is on the left, as seen in 1911.

186 Queen's Park war memorial was in Beethoven Street, and this scene shows a crowded Armistice Day in the 1920s, but it became disused and untended until it was rescued by local residents and proudly refixed in the hall of the Beethoven Centre.

Bibliography

Ainsworth, W Harrison, *Jack Sheppard* (1839), *Old St Paul's* (1841)

Ball, Stanley, *Notes for talk on Old Willesden* (1895)

Barker, T.C., and Robbins, Michael, *A History of London Transport* (1974)

Barres-Baker, M.C., *Places in Brent: Harlesden, Kensal Green* (undated)

Beeson, Amos (ed. by Cliff Wadsworth), *Harlesden Green in the 1870s* (1996)

Bolitho, Hector (ed.), *A Batsford Centenary 1843-1943* (1943)

Brock, Dr Richard E., *A History of Kilburn Grammar School* (1985)

Burnett, John, *A Social History of Housing* (1986)

Clunn, Harold P, *The Face of London* (1951

Cole, G.D.H. and Postgate, Raymond, *The Common People 1746-1946* (1971, reprint)

Cummins, Mark, (ed.), *Queen's Park Centenary Brochure 1997-1987* (1987)

Guinness, Edward, *The Guinness Book of Guinness* (1988)

Jackson, A.A., *Semi-Detached London* (1985)

Jewish Chronicle (1905)

Kelly's Directory of Willesden (various dates from 1972 to 1923)

Leff, Vera and Blunden G.H., *The Willesden Story* (1965)

Lysons, D., *The Environs of London, Vol 3* (1795)

McDonald, Erica and Smith Donald T., *Artizans and Avenues* (2004)

Macey, Gordon, *Queen's Park Rangers* (1993)

Morris, John, *Domesday Book – Middlesex* (1975)

Passmore Edwards, J., *A Few Footprints* (1905)

Potter, Simeon, *The Story of Willesden* (1926)

Robbins, Michael, *Middlesex* (1953)

Snow, Len, *Well Done – the Story of Willesden Hospital* (2006)

Snow, Len, *Willesden Past* (1994)

Soulsby, Lucy, *Brondesbury Ways* (1916)

Victoria County History, Vol VII, Willesden (1982), *Vol IX Paddington* (1989)

Wadsworth, Cliff, *Traditional Pubs of Brent – Vol. 1 Willesden* (1999), *Robson the Roadmaker* (1997), (ed.) *Beating the Bounds – A Walk around the Willesden Boundary* (2000)

Willesden Chronicle (various dates)
Willesden History Society Journals (1990 to date)
Willesden Illustrated Monthly (1937)
Wood, F.A., Dexter, B.W. and Ball, S. (eds), *The Parish of Willesden* (1872 onwards)

Index

Numbers in **bold** refer to the illustrations, otherwise they are page numbers